VELOCITY™

DAREDEVILS' GUIDES

A DAREDEVIL'S GUIDE TO STORM CHASING

by Amie Jane Leavitt

Consultant:
Joshua Wurman
Center for Severe Weather Research
Boulder, Colorado

CAPSTONE PRESS
a capstone imprint

Velocity Books are published by Capstone Press,
1710 Roe Crest Drive, North Mankato, Minnesota 56003
www.capstonepub.com

Library of Congress Cataloging-in-Publication Data
Leavitt, Amie Jane, author.
A daredevil's guide to storm chasing / by Amie Jane Leavitt.
pages cm. — (Velocity. Daredevils' guides)
Audience: 8-13
Audience: Grade 4 to 6
Summary: "Describes the activity of storm chasing, including how it's done, the dangers
involved, and how it has helped scientists learn about severe weather"—Provided
by publisher.
Includes bibliographical references and index.
ISBN 978-1-4296-9984-6 (library binding)
ISBN 978-1-4765-1804-6 (ebook PDF)
1. Tornadoes—Juvenile literature. 2. Severe storms—Juvenile literature. 3. Storm chasers—
Juvenile literature. I. Title.
QC955.2.L43 2013
511.55'3—dc23   2012020518

Editorial Credits
Carrie Braulick Sheely, editor; Veronica Correia, designer; Wanda Winch, media
researcher; Laura Manthe, production specialist

Photo Credits
©Jack Elston, University of Colorado Boulder, 33 (top); © University Corporation for
Atmospheric Research (UCAR), 23 (t); Basehunters: Kevin Rolfs, 11 (bottom right);
Center for Severe Weather Research (CSWR), 33 (middle right), Andrew Arnold, 32 (r),
coloradowebs.com, 32 (mr); Corbis: Jim Reed, 8-9, 30, 33 (bottom left), 38-39; Courtesy
of David K. Hoadley, 27; Discovery Channel, 21 (b), 44 (l); Dreamstime: Benjamin Todd
Shoemake, 28-29, Rob Stegmann, 11 (ml); George Kourounis, www.stormchaser.ca., 6, 7,
11 (bl); Jeremy Shields, greatplainstornadotours.com, 11 (t); Marcie Spence, 18-19; NASA,
12 (m), 34; National Geographic Stock: Annie Griffiths Belt, 35, Carsten Peter, 40-41, 42-43;
NOAA, 22-23, 29 (tr), Mike Coniglio, 4-5, 33 (br), NSSL, 11 (mr), 24 (inset), 33 (ml), NWS,
reference,10 (all); Photo courtesy of (Sharon Watson), the Kansas Adjutant General's
Department, Topeka, Kansas, 45; Shutterstock: Alexey Kashin, 32 (l), Bocos Benedict, 10-11
(back), Bruce Rolff, cover (m), 1, Chris Hellyar, 26, cobalt88, 20 (br), Eky Studio, 6-7 (back),
ElaValo, 20 (mr), HuHu, 37 (t), Joel Calheiros, cover (t), 12-13 (back), Leonello Calvetti, 16
(b), Leshik, cover (br), Nataliia Natykach, 18-19 (back), 20-21 (back), notkoo, 34 (l), obradart,
26-27 (back), photobank.kiev.ua, cover (tr), back cover, 36-37 (back), prudkov, abstract line
background, Ra Studio, 20 (t), rangizzz, 20 (ml), Sascha Burkard, 44 (tree), soll, 31, Toria,
10-11 (back), Tribalium, 28 (tl), Yuriy Ponomarev, 4 (bl); SuperStock Inc: age fotostock, 37 (b);
Texas Tech University, 32 (ml); Tim Samaras, 21 (t); U.S. Air Force: Tech Sgt. Ryan Labadens,
24-25

Printed in the United States of America in Stevens Point, Wisconsin.
092012   006937WZS13

Table of Contents

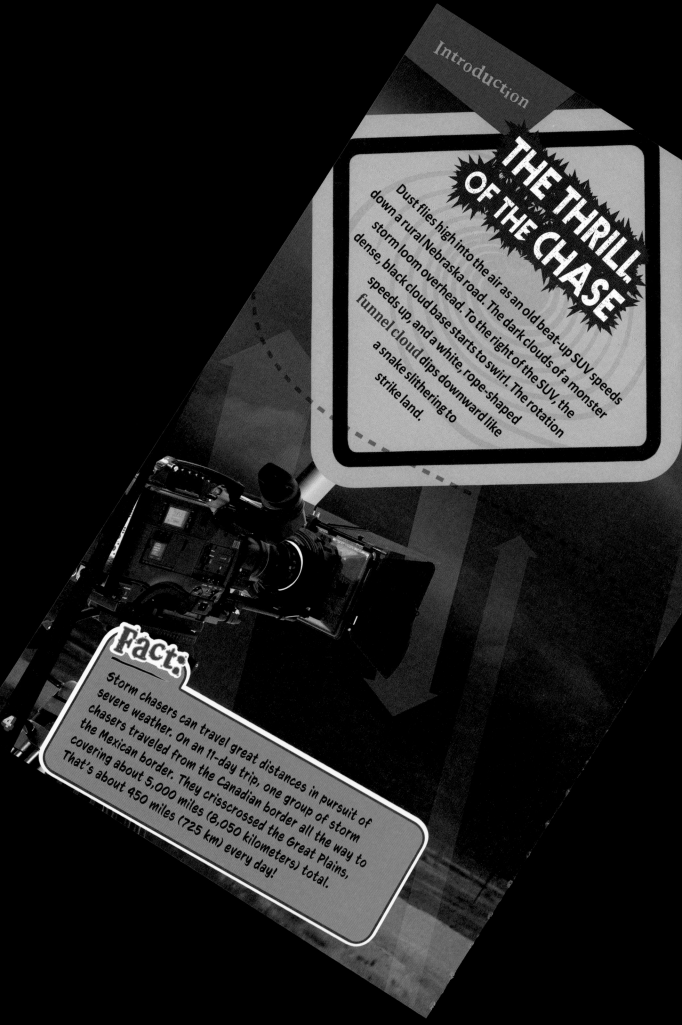

THE THRILL OF THE CHASE

Dust flies high into the air as an old beat-up SUV speeds down a rural Nebraska road. The dark clouds of a monster storm loom overhead. To the right of the SUV, the dense, black cloud base starts to swirl. The rotation speeds up, and a white, rope-shaped funnel cloud dips downward like a snake slithering to strike land.

Fact:

Storm chasers can travel great distances in pursuit of severe weather. On an 11-day trip, one group of storm chasers traveled from the Canadian border all the way to the Mexican border. They crisscrossed the Great Plains, covering about 5,000 miles (8,050 kilometers) total. That's about 450 miles (725 km) every day!

4

"Pull over!" the passenger yells. The driver slams on the brakes and stops alongside the road. The passenger grabs his video camera and hops out of the car. The driver runs to the back of the vehicle to set up a storm-measuring tornado pod.

The long, skinny funnel cloud sways back and forth as if it's deciding which part of the land to strike. Finally, it lashes out and hits an area of open grassland.

"Tornado!" the passenger yells while getting a close-up view of the storm with his camera. The driver places a pod in the field, directly in what they hope will be the tornado's path. Then the long tornado gets wider and wider and seems to barrel right for them. It sounds like a huge freight train is about to roll over the top of them.

"It's coming our way! Let's get going!"

The two storm chasers rush into the SUV and race forward. Behind them, the tornado spins along the open field, flinging dirt and debris. It changes colors from white to brown to black. At last, it spins right over the top of the tornado pod, just as the chasers had hoped. "Impact!" yells the passenger. "We did it!"

In 2009 and 2010, more than 150 scientists from the Vortex2 project chased storms in the central United States. In May and June 2009, the Vortex2 team traveled more than 10,000 miles (16,100 km).

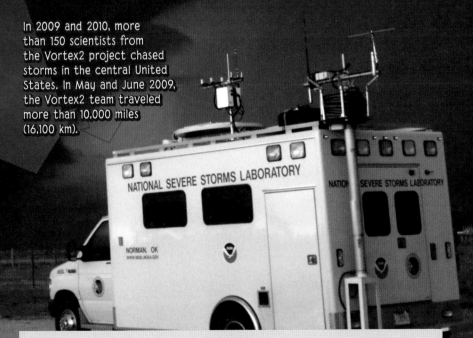

funnel cloud—a cloud that hangs from a larger storm cloud but has not touched the ground; funnel clouds often have rotation and precede a tornado

tornado—a violent spinning column of air that makes contact with the ground

INTO NATURE'S FURY

Most people run for shelter when they hear the wail of storm warning sirens. But not storm chasers. When they hear warning sirens, they are often already in the heart of the action.

Storm chasers are people who actively pursue any kind of severe weather, including thunderstorms, tornadoes, hurricanes, and blizzards. Most storm chasers pursue tornadoes and hurricanes since these are the most dramatic storms. Storm chasers generally "chase" tornadoes, thunderstorms, and blizzards and "hunt or study" hurricanes.

It takes a special kind of daredevil to race into the heart of nature's fury. Who are these people and why do they chase? You're about to find out the answers to these questions and more.

tornado in Texas, 2005

Fact:

The Drake Passage between the tips of South America and Antarctica is an attraction for storm chasers. High-speed winds rush through the waterway, causing monster waves.

Storm Spotters vs. Storm Chasers

They have similar names, but storm spotters and storm chasers are very different. Storm spotters are people trained by the National Weather Service (NWS) to watch for severe weather in their local area. They then report storm information to the NWS. The NWS uses the information gathered by spotters to make more accurate minute-by-minute weather reports. Storm spotters rarely leave their home areas. Storm chasers hunt down storms and try to get as close to them as safely possible. They often drive hundreds of miles to hunt down the wildest and biggest storms.

Q & A WITH STORM CHASER REBEKAH LaBAR

QUESTION: What do you love the most about storm chasing?

ANSWER: You never know what you are going to see when you go chasing. Every tornado is different, every storm is different, and I love to chase every opportunity I get in search of more beautiful and exciting storms. I have a great interest in photography and videography, so I am always in search of photogenic storms and tornadoes on the [Great] Plains. Also, as a meteorologist, I take great pride in making a good forecast and then having that forecast verified in the form of tornadoes in my target area. Another reason I like storm chasing is the fun I have with my friends while driving all day in the Great Plains.

A storm chaser experiences the power of Hurricane Igor in Bermuda in September 2010.

THE DRIVING FORCE

WHAT MOTIVATES PEOPLE TO RUN HEAD-ON INTO
NATURE'S MOST EXTREME STORMS?
The answers are just as varied as the storm chasers themselves.

The Thrill of the Chase

Chasing severe weather can be exciting. The same kind of feeling
that people get doing dangerous activities like skydiving can also
be felt on a storm chase. This feeling of danger keeps storm chasers
searching for the "perfect" storm.

Scientific Research

Storm chasers may not be out there just for the excitement. Some
chasers are on missions to gather scientific data. Although much is
known about tornadoes and tornado prediction, some things remain
a mystery. For example, scientists would like to learn exactly what
causes a funnel cloud to reach the ground. Scientific storm chasers
use special weather equipment to gather information. They also take
photos and record videos to study later.

Some chasers contact the National Weather Service when they
see thunderstorms to help the organization make public warnings
more accurate. But while this feedback can be helpful, scientists
who chase thunderstorms mainly collect data to improve future
warning systems.

Unlike the data from thunderstorm chasers, the information
from hurricane hunters affects daily forecasts immediately.
Hurricane hunters in planes gather information about wind speed,
air pressure, and air temperature in the storm. They fly in and out
of hurricanes and send their data immediately back to the National
Hurricane Center. This information helps scientists properly track a
hurricane so officials can warn people in the storm's path.

Catching the Shot

News media organizations pay for storm photos and videos. The money provides motivation for some storm chasers. However, news outlets only buy the best photos and videos. They want the most dramatic and unusual shots. For this reason, storm chasers often push the limits to get as close as possible to nature's fury.

Marveling Nature

Severe weather varies, and chasers can never know what to expect. One day they might see a tornado 1 mile (1.6 km) wide. Another day they might see a **storm surge** as tall as a two-story building crash onto shore. Looking at a picture of one of these storms is simply not the same as seeing it yourself. This is yet another reason why people are drawn to storm chasing. They want to see nature in all its glory. Storm chaser David Hoadley says, "Few life experiences can compare with standing in hard, gusting wind and looking up at a developing tornado ..."

air pressure—the force exerted by the weight of the molecules that make up air; usually, the lower the air pressure, the stronger the storm

storm surge—a huge wave of water pushed ashore by an approaching hurricane

Chapter 1

THE INS AND OUTS OF MONSTER STORMS

Twirling Winds and Flying Debris

Many storm chasers are looking for one specific thing—a tornado. Tornadoes form inside thunderstorms, yet not every thunderstorm forms tornadoes. Large storms called supercells are most likely to cause tornadoes. Scientists are still learning why some thunderstorms produce tornadoes while others do not. Out of every five or six supercells, only one produces a tornado. What experts do know is that tornadoes need certain types of air to form:

- warm, moist air near the ground
- cool, dry air in the upper **atmosphere**
- fast-moving winds that blow in different directions at different **altitudes**

How a Tornado Forms

A thunderstorm is developing. If the wind changes direction and speed with increasing height, the air may begin spinning horizontally in the lower atmosphere.

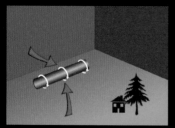

When the warm air rises, it may push one end of the rotating air column higher. If this happens, the column will no longer be spinning horizontally. Instead, it will be spinning vertically. This vertical spinning air is called a mesocyclone. One end of the mesocyclone points down toward the ground.

The area of rotation could be between 2 and 6 miles (3.2 and 9.7 km) wide. Through a process not entirely understood by scientists, sometimes the mesocyclone forms a tornado.

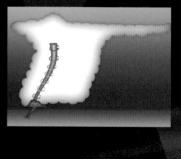

Tornado Shapes

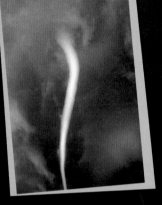

A **WEDGE TORNADO** is wide and short. It is almost triangular in shape and looks like a slice of pie.

A **ROPE TORNADO** is narrow and thin. It looks like a long rope or a snake.

An **ELEPHANT TRUNK TORNADO** is wider than a rope tornado. Its tapered shape often curves down toward the ground, resembling an elephant's trunk.

A **STOVEPIPE TORNADO** has a thick funnel that goes straight down to the ground. It looks like a big tube or pipe.

A **CONE TORNADO** is wide at the top. It comes down to the ground in a shape that looks like an ice-cream cone.

atmosphere—the mixture of gases that surrounds Earth
altitude—the height of something above a surface, such as sea level or the ground

A SPINNING STORM WITH A CALM EYE

Hurricane hunters aim their planes into the center of thick, spinning walls of clouds. They brave severe thunderstorms that shake and rattle their planes. But all of this is done to make more accurate forecasts.

Hurricanes form over warm water in areas where the air is warm and moist. They have high wind speeds of at least 74 miles (119 km) per hour. Like tornadoes, hurricanes have wind rotation. They spin around a center **eye**.

A hurricane needs fuel to survive. It gets this fuel from the warm ocean water. Hurricanes form over water that has a temperature of at least 80 degrees Fahrenheit (27 degrees Celsius) for at least the first 165 feet (50 meters) of depth.

Dry air sinks down into the center of the storm.

The calm eye usually has clear skies. The warm air sinking into the eye prevents cloud formation. The eye's warm temperature gives it a very low air pressure.

Warm, moist air is drawn into the storm. This air provides fuel for the storm.

Water vapor evaporates from the ocean. As it rises, the water vapor cools and condenses. This condensation forms clouds.

The eyewall is the most violent part of the storm. Wind speed and rainfall are the most intense here.

Fact:

The Earth's rotation causes the rotation in tropical disturbances. The equator divides the Earth into northern and southern hemispheres. Storms move in a counterclockwise direction in the northern hemisphere. They move in a clockwise direction in the southern hemisphere. There is no spin of wind on the equator. For this reason, hurricanes cannot form less than 300 miles (480 km) from it.

Birth of a Hurricane

Storms progress into hurricanes in several stages. Each stage has a different name.

1. Tropical Disturbance

a storm that begins in warm, tropical waters
- heavy clouds and rain present for at least 24 hours
- storm slightly rotates

2. Tropical Depression

a rotating storm with a long-lasting surface wind of less than 39 miles (63 km) per hour

3. Tropical Storm

a rotating storm with a long-lasting surface wind speed of 39 to 73 miles (63 to 117 km) per hour

4. Hurricane

a rotating storm with a long-lasting surface wind speed of at least 74 miles (119 km) per hour

One Storm, Many Names

Hurricanes are known by different names depending on where they form. They are called hurricanes in the northern hemisphere's Atlantic and eastern Pacific Oceans. In the northern hemisphere's western Pacific Ocean, they are called typhoons. In the southern hemisphere, hurricanes are known as tropical cyclones.

Hurricane

Tropical Cyclone

Typhoon

eye—the central, calm area at the center of a hurricane
evaporate—to change from a liquid into a vapor or a gas
condense—to change from gas to liquid; water vapor condenses into liquid water
eyewall—a tall, vertical wall of fast-moving clouds surrounding a hurricane's eye

TORNADO ALLEY

The United States is the storm chasing capital of the world. Australian storm chaser Jimmy Deguara says that the main difference between the United States and the rest of the world is the tornado. "In the U.S., there are days where you are almost guaranteed to find tornadoes," Deguara says, "and the storms are absolutely phenomenal."

More tornadoes occur in the United States than in any other country. Tornadoes do form in other places, but they're much rarer. Tornadoes have struck every state. Yet some states experience more tornadoes than others. These states are found in the Great Plains region in an area known as Tornado Alley. Tornado Alley is prone to tornadoes because warm, moist air from the Gulf of Mexico moves north. Thunderstorms are more likely to develop when warm, moist air is present. Strong eastward-moving winds traveling through the region also make tornadoes more likely to form in the region. There is no agreed-upon boundary of Tornado Alley. However, it usually includes Kansas, Oklahoma, Nebraska, South Dakota, and Texas. Most tornadoes hit Tornado Alley during spring.

Ranking Tornadoes

In 1971 meteorologist Dr. Tetsuya Theodore Fujita developed the six-category Fujita (F) Scale. This scale grouped tornadoes based on the damage they caused. After viewing the damage, scientists estimated the tornado's wind speed. In 2007 the Enhanced Fujita (EF) Scale replaced the F Scale. The EF Scale groups tornadoes the same way the F Scale did. But the EF Scale takes a bigger variety of materials and building structure types into account. It also has greatly reduced wind speeds for each category. About 30 percent of U.S. tornadoes are between EF0 and EF2. Only about 2 percent of U.S. tornadoes reach the EF4 or EF5 stage.

The EF Scale

EF Number	Degree of Damage	3-second wind gust estimate (miles per hour)
EF0	light	65-85
EF1	moderate	86-110
EF2	considerable	111-135
EF3	severe	136-165
EF4	devastating	166-200
EF5	incredible	more than 200

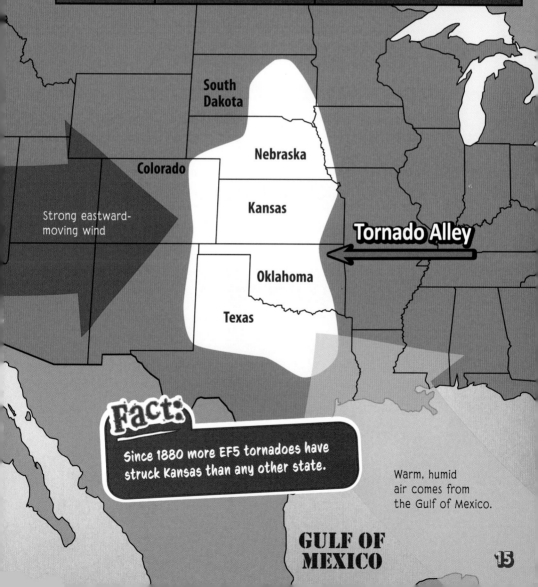

South Dakota

Nebraska

Colorado

Kansas

Strong eastward-moving wind

Tornado Alley

Oklahoma

Texas

Fact:
Since 1880 more EF5 tornadoes have struck Kansas than any other state.

Warm, humid air comes from the Gulf of Mexico.

GULF OF MEXICO

HURRICANE ALLEY

Similar to Tornado Alley, an area of the Atlantic Ocean is known for having a high number of hurricanes. This area is called Hurricane Alley. It stretches from western Africa to the eastern U.S. coast. Hurricanes that form off the coast of western Africa roll across the region like balls in a bowling alley. They gain strength as they move across the warm ocean water. Sometimes they strike the Caribbean Islands, Bahamas, and Central America. Sometimes they hit Florida and the southeastern U.S. coast. Other times, they bounce up the U.S. coast. Hurricanes from Hurricane Alley have hit areas as far north as New England. In 2011 Hurricane Irene caused a great deal of damage in Vermont. In 2012 Hurricane Sandy caused major damage up and down the East Coast.

Hurricane season in Hurricane Alley generally runs from June 1 to November 30. But most hurricanes form from August to mid-October. It's most likely that a hurricane from this area would strike land in mid-September. At this time of year, the water is warmest. The warm water makes it more likely that a tropical storm would reach hurricane strength.

United States

Hurricane Alley

Africa

Saffir-Simpson Scale

Herbert Saffir and Bob Simpson developed the five-category Saffir-Simpson scale in 1969. This scale groups hurricanes according to their wind speed. The scale includes the types of damage that people can expect with each group. Hurricanes are put into a category soon after they form.

Category	Wind Speed (miles per hour)	Damage	Example
Category 1	74 to 95 mph (119 to 153 kph)	minor damage to trees and mobile homes	Hurricane Isaac, 2012
Category 2	96 to 110 mph (154 to 177 kph)	major damage to mobile homes and minor damage to small buildings	Hurricane Alex, 2010
Category 3	111 to 130 mph (179 to 209 kph)	moderate damage to small buildings; some trees uprooted or snapped	Hurricane Karl, 2010
Category 4	131 to 155 mph (211 to 249 kph)	major damage to small buildings; many trees uprooted or snapped	Hurricane Ophelia, 2011
Category 5	> 155 mph (> 249 kph)	extreme damage to or destruction of buildings and trees	Hurricane Katrina, 2005

Hurricane Naming System

Hurricanes are named using an alphabetical list of 21 names. The first storm is given an A name, the second a B name, and so forth. Hurricane names alternate between male and female names. Most names are reused every six years. But the names of hurricanes that have caused severe damage, such as Hurricane Andrew and Hurricane Katrina, are retired. They will never be used again to name a hurricane.

Chapter 2

VEHICLES AND TOOLS OF THE CHASE

Twister-worthy Autos

Mammoth-sized vehicles and decked-out vans aren't necessary to storm chase. Most chasers drive around in cars and SUVs. However, some teams have designed special vehicles for storm chasing. These vehicles allow them to get close to storms while staying safe.

Filmmaker Sean Casey designed the TIV 2 for his storm documentary. It's like a movable tripod weighing

14,000 pounds (6,350 kilograms). The TIV 2 allows the team to get close to a tornado so Casey can film it from the turret on the vehicle's roof.

To build the TIV 2, Casey and his crew used a Dodge Ram 3500 pickup truck as a frame. Then they made all of the changes to turn it into an armored "tornado tank."

Safety flaps slide down to the ground to keep wind from blowing underneath the vehicle and tipping it over.

A large diesel engine gives the TIV 2 plenty of power. It can push the vehicle to a top speed of about 100 miles (161 km) per hour.

A steel spike on each side of the TIV 2 can be lowered 40 inches (102 cm) into the ground. The spikes stabilize the vehicle in a storm.

The vehicle sits high off the ground. Its position helps it travel on unpaved roads without getting stuck.

Fact:

TIV stands for Tornado Intercept Vehicle. TIV 1 was designed in 2003. It was built on the frame of a 1997 Ford F-450 pickup truck.

QUESTION: Are certain vehicles better than others for storm chasing?

ANSWER: Most chasers use SUVs, mainly for the fact that they sit higher off the road, have better visibility, and several people can ride along. But I've seen chasers in vans, pickup trucks, and four-door sedans. There's even one chaser I know of that drives a Prius (a small car). And, of course, there are big custom storm chasing "tanks" like the TIV and the Dominator. I chase in a 2007 Pontiac Torrent, which is a small SUV.

The camera turret can move in a full circle. The full rotation allows Casey to get complete pictures of storms.

The instrument mast collects data, including wind speed and relative humidity.

TIV 2's protective armor is made of strong materials, such as steel, Kevlar, and a very sturdy plastic called polycarb. The armor protects the vehicle from flying debris.

TIV 2 has a 92-gallon (348-liter) fuel tank. It can travel about 750 miles (1,200 km) between fill-ups.

All of the wheels can be put into four-wheel drive to help the vehicle travel in mud.

relative humidity—the ratio of the amount of water vapor present in the air to the maximum amount that can exist in vapor form at that specific temperature and pressure

Storm Chasing Gear

Early storm chasers had very basic equipment compared to today's chasers. Early chasers generally used two-way radios, a street map, and their eyes to find storms. Today chasers must still use their eyes and their brains. Many chasers still use two-way radios too. But modern chasers also use high-tech gadgets. Most modern chasers use these basics:

Laptop Computer

A laptop computer with Internet access is one of the most important tools modern storm chasers use. It allows chasers to receive continual updates from the National Weather Service. As they watch radar images on the screen, chasers are able to determine which thunderstorms are most likely to cause tornadoes. The laptop also allows chasers to immediately upload their storm photos and videos to the Internet. This capability gives people around the world the chance to see the action as it's happening. Laptops are also used to report tornado sightings. "I use a computer application called Spotter Network to report tornadoes," says Skip Talbot, a storm chaser from Chicago. "I type up my report and it gets sent with my GPS location to the NWS office automatically."

Smartphone

A smartphone is a cell phone with Internet and GPS capabilities. Internet access allows chasers to report tornado sightings to the NWS. Chasers can also upload photos and videos from their phones to websites. Using GPS, the phone can provide chasers with specific travel directions to a certain location. In addition to their smartphones, chasers may have GPS navigation in their cars.

Odds and Ends

- binoculars
- first-aid kit
- flashlight
- travel chargers for cell phones and computers

Photography Equipment

A camera that takes still pictures and video allows chasers to record storm details. Most chasers use digital cameras.

Devices called tornado probes take measurements inside tornadoes. In 1997 Tim Samaras developed a special kind of tornado probe called a HITPR "turtle" probe. His probe was shaped differently from earlier turtle probes. Previous probes were shaped similar to salad bowls. They lifted easily. The HITPR probe looked more like a flattened cone. Its shape protected it from being flung by a tornado's wind.

Samaras' probe took the turtle probe to a whole new level. Samaras was an engineer and an explosives expert. He used his knowledge to design a probe that could withstand a tornado's violent power. When a tornado passes over his probe, the device measures how much the air pressure drops inside the storm. The probe also measures the humidity level, air temperature, wind speed, and wind direction.

QUESTION: How long have you been using your turtle probes?

ANSWER: As of 2012 my probes have been in the field now for 12 years. I've been able to successfully deploy them in tornadoes every year.

QUESTION: What do you feel is the most important information you have obtained from your turtle probes so far?

ANSWER: We were able to validate the extreme pressure drop inside a tornado.

QUESTION: Do you personally analyze the data from your turtle probes?

ANSWER: Yes. we analyze the data by using other data sources such as radar. satellite, and surface observations. We draw conclusions based on what we collect and either prove or disprove theories.

Tim Samaras

radar—a system that uses radio waves to detect and locate objects

GPS—an electronic tool that uses satellites to find the location of an object; GPS stands for Global Positioning System

humidity—the measure of the moisture in the air

satellite—a spacecraft that circles Earth; satellites take pictures of Earth from space

HUNTING IN THE AIR

Satellite images provide important information about the path of a hurricane. However, satellites cannot detect the wind speed inside the hurricane or the interior air pressure of the storm. The only way that information can be gathered is by flying into the storm. The National Oceanic and Atmospheric Administration (NOAA) hurricane hunters fly the Lockheed WP-3 Orion into the heart of a hurricane. They fly the Gulfstream IV-SP jet on the outside of a hurricane. The U.S. Air Force Reserve hurricane hunters fly the Lockheed C-130 Hercules through a hurricane.

WP-3 Orion

ELECTRONICS: The electronic equipment is stored in the plane's midsection. Technicians continually monitor the equipment during flights.

NOSE RADAR: The crew members use the nose radar to monitor weather conditions in front of them.

BELLY RADAR: This radar allows the crew to see weather that is in front of, behind, and to the sides of the plane.

WINGSPAN (FROM ONE WINGTIP TO THE OTHER): 99 feet, 8 inches (30.4 meters)

LENGTH: 116 feet, 10 inches (35.4 meters)

The Dropsonde

The dropsonde sends information back to the aircraft every 0.5 seconds by GPS. The scientists send this data and other information to the National Hurricane Center. Hurricane hunters use more than 4,000 dropsondes each year.

DROPSONDE STATION: During flight the crew releases measuring devices called dropsondes. The dropsondes collect key information about the hurricane, such as air temperature, wind speed, and air pressure.

TAIL RADAR: The tail radar allows the crew to see the weather that is behind, above, and below the plane.

TURBOPROP ENGINES: These four engines are designed to be used in severe weather. Turboprops have a propeller, while jet engines do not. Turboprops withstand heavy rain and strong winds better than jet engines. Hurricane hunters must travel slowly through hurricanes. Turboprops are better suited for traveling at slower speeds than jet engines.

Fact:

Since the first flight into a hurricane in 1944, four planes have been lost. Thirty-six people died in these crashes.

PREPARING FOR THE JOB

The brain can be the most important piece of equipment a storm chaser has. Before storm chasers get into their vehicles, they spend a great deal of time improving their skills and studying.

Many storm chasers have degrees in meteorology. A degree isn't required to be a storm chaser. But chasers must have a great deal of knowledge about meteorology. Chasers must understand clouds and their formations to stay safe. They also have to know how to read radar maps and use weather equipment. "Going out there without the necessary knowledge and experience can be very dangerous. You're liable to find yourself right in the path of very large hail or even worse, a tornado," says storm chaser Chris McBee.

Radar maps from the National Weather Service look like an art project gone wild. But all of the colored blobs show where storms are developing, where lightning is striking, and where tornadoes could develop.

Hurricane Hunters of the U.S. Air Force

Many hurricane hunters are professional pilots, scientists, and navigators. They often have advanced experience with aircraft and meteorology. Getting a career in this field is definitely not easy. If you want to be part of the U.S. Air Force Reserve 53rd Weather Reconnaissance Squadron, here's what you have to do.

1. Finish high school. If you want an officer position, you also need a four-year degree. Hurricane hunter officer positions include navigators, pilots, and weather officers.

2. Take a military qualification test to join the Air Force Reserve.

3. Interview for the position.

4. Pass a flight physical. All flight positions require that you pass this physical. You must meet the vision requirements. You must have good hearing, low blood pressure, and overall good health. In addition, you need to meet weight standards.

5. Be accepted by the review board (for pilots and navigators only).

6. Complete military training. Non-officers complete basic military training. Officers attend officer training school.

7. Flight positions require a three-day course. During this training researchers will see how your body reacts to the stresses of flight.

8. Complete formal training. Several crew positions require full-time training. This training will teach you how to do a certain job on the aircraft. The training can last from a few months to a year.

9. Complete survival school. Every air crew member receives survival training. It covers survival skills in mountains as well as in the water.

10. Complete qualification training. Specialized training is provided for new hurricane hunters.

Fact:

Many storm chasers who race after tornadoes also drive into the paths of hurricanes. This allows them to see what it's like when the huge storms hit land.

25

Chapter 3

A HAIR-RAISING HISTORY

A Chase to Remember

It was a warm afternoon on May 25, 1965. David Hoadley hopped into his maroon 1962 Ford Falcon and headed west toward Dodge City, Kansas. He had been chasing storms in the Great Plains for several years. The previous summer he had seen a few funnel clouds from afar. But he longed to see a really big tornado and capture it on film. Even though he was living on the East Coast now, his desire to chase was still as strong as ever. David was in search of the "perfect" tornado.

Today looked like it might be the day he'd see one. Around 1:00 p.m., the regular radio programming was interrupted with a special alert. Warning! Tornado! Take shelter! David saw storm clouds filling the southern sky. He sped south, directly into the path of the storm. As he neared the town of Minneola, he saw a thin, white rope tornado snaking across the sky about 20 miles (32 km) away. David then turned east to follow a line of thunderstorms.

Hoadley used a Mamiyaflex camera for his 1965 tornado shot. These twin-lens cameras were first sold in the late 1940s.

Just as he neared the west side of the town of Pratt, David saw several cars parked alongside the road. People were nervously staring up at the sky. David parked next to a highway patrol officer. Then he hurried out of the car, clutching his camera firmly.

Lightning lit up the sky in the southwest. Deep thunder rumbled. Suddenly, about 3 miles (4.8 km) to the north, a smooth-sided cone-shaped funnel cloud began descending from the cloud base. It snaked out of the sky and hit the ground. At this distance, the tornado was silent. The only sounds were the distant wails of Pratt's warning sirens and the officer's voice reporting from the scene.

David quickly snapped a photo of the spinning cone. Yet when he finished, he worried that his shaking hands had ruined the shot. So he steadied the camera on the car's hood and carefully took another. This one was the best shot of the day. Even after 47 years, David still remembered this event vividly in 2012. "It was like an oil painting appearing on a giant canvas," he recalls.

With this successful chase, David became a part of storm chasing history without realizing it. He became known as the first storm chaser to cross state lines.

David Hoadley's 1965 tornado shot

Fact:

The tornado that struck near Pratt, Kansas, on May 25, 1965, was an F3 tornado. Eight people were injured in the twister.

HOW IT ALL BEGAN

Tracing the history of storm chasing is not exact. Early chasers often didn't record their activities. But there are still plenty of noteworthy events in storm chasing.

Big Moments in Storm Chasing History

1743

Benjamin Franklin chases a whirlwind on horseback for almost a mile. It is the first documented storm chase in history. Years later, in 1752, he conducts his famous electricity experiment by flying a kite in a thunderstorm.

JULY 27, 1943

Air Force colonel Joe Duckworth becomes the first pilot to fly a plane into a hurricane. He did so after betting fellow pilots that he could do it.

SEPT. 1945

The U.S. War Department establishes the 53rd Weather Reconnaissance Squadron. This group's mission is to get information about hurricanes by flying directly into them.

1952

The U.S. Weather Bureau issues its first tornado forecasts.

1953

Roger Jensen begins chasing and photographing storms in his home state of North Dakota. He becomes one of the first people to chase storms as a hobby.

MAY 4, 1961

Neil B. Ward chases a thunderstorm with many tornadoes near Geary, Oklahoma. He reports it to the Weather Bureau using a police car's radio. Ward eventually becomes one of the country's top tornado scientists.

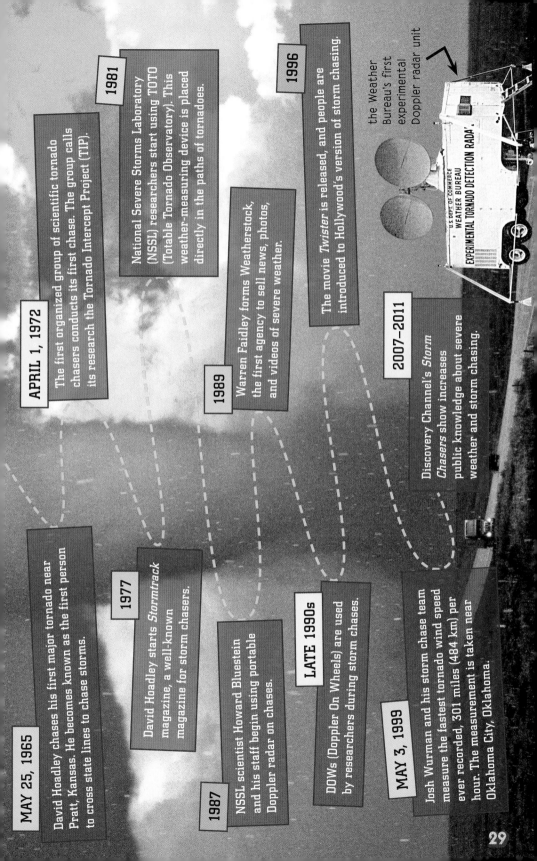

MAY 25, 1965

David Hoadley chases his first major tornado near Pratt, Kansas. He becomes known as the first person to cross state lines to chase storms.

APRIL 1, 1972

The first organized group of scientific tornado chasers conducts its first chase. The group calls its research the Tornado Intercept Project (TIP).

1977

David Hoadley starts *Stormtrack* magazine, a well-known magazine for storm chasers.

1981

National Severe Storms Laboratory (NSSL) researchers start using TOTO (Totable Tornado Observatory). This weather-measuring device is placed directly in the paths of tornadoes.

1987

NSSL scientist Howard Bluestein and his staff begin using portable Doppler radar on chases.

1989

Warren Faidley forms Weatherstock, the first agency to sell news, photos, and videos of severe weather.

1996

The movie *Twister* is released, and people are introduced to Hollywood's version of storm chasing.

LATE 1990s

DOWs (Doppler On Wheels) are used by researchers during storm chases.

MAY 3, 1999

Josh Wurman and his storm chase team measure the fastest tornado wind speed ever recorded, 301 miles (484 km) per hour. The measurement is taken near Oklahoma City, Oklahoma.

2007–2011

Discovery Channel's *Storm Chasers* show increases public knowledge about severe weather and storm chasing.

the Weather Bureau's first experimental Doppler radar unit

U.S DEPT OF COMMERCE
WEATHER BUREAU
EXPERIMENTAL TORNADO DETECTION RADAR

THE VORTEX2 PROJECT

Vortex2 was the largest storm chase project in history.
During 2009 and 2010, more than 150 scientists collected data.
They used more than 40 specially equipped vehicles.

VORTEX2 IS AN ACRONYM THAT STANDS FOR:
Verification of the
Origin of
Rotation in
Tornadoes
Experiment
2 the second Vortex project
(VORTEX1 was conducted in 1994 and 1995.)

who was involved?

Vortex2 combined the efforts of scientists and college students from around the United States and the world. Participating organizations included:

- National Severe Storms Laboratory (part of NOAA)
- National Center for Atmospheric Research
- National Science Foundation
- Center for Severe Weather Research
- a number of universities with highly respected meteorology programs

How much did it cost?

This U.S. government project cost more than $12 million.

Goals

The purpose of the Vortex2 project was to gather information about supercells and tornadoes using specialized equipment. Team members hoped the information would allow them to re-create an accurate computer model of a tornado.

The team also hoped to learn enough about tornadoes to improve tornado warning systems. Right now, people only get warnings about 11 minutes before a tornado strikes—if they're lucky. Scientists would like to increase that amount of time. Eventually, they'd like to give people 20-minute, 30-minute, or even 50-minute warnings. Vortex2 scientists also hoped they could help make tornado warnings more accurate. Currently about 70 percent of tornado warnings are false alarms. With so many false alarms, people may ignore them. Ignoring warnings can be very dangerous if a tornado does hit.

What Happened?

The Vortex2 team chased and intercepted a total of 20 tornadoes. However, they only caught one tornado in the entire 2009 season. This might sound like a disappointment. But this one tornado ended up being the most documented tornado capture in history. It happened on June 5, 2009, in Goshen County, Wyoming.

On this day, the Vortex2 team was in the right place at the right time. Because of that, scientists were able to watch the entire life cycle of the storm. They watched it from its formation until it died out—a total of 25 minutes. During that time, they used many weather instruments to gather data. Nothing like this had ever been done before.

HOW TO CATCH A THUNDERSTORM

Storm chase teams use a variety of strategies to hunt down storms. Hobbyist chasers often use minimal equipment and their own personal knowledge. Advanced scientific teams use dozens of vehicles with high-tech equipment. The Vortex2 team was one of these groups. The vehicle or gear the scientists used depended on what distance they were from the storm. Other research projects continue to use Vortex2 equipment, such as DOWs and tornado pods.

Sticknets are sturdy tripods about 6.5 feet (2 m) tall. They collect a variety of data near the ground.

Tornado pods measure wind **velocity**, wind direction, and other weather data inside a tornado. They are placed directly in a tornado's path.

The short-band radar truck stays within 3 miles (4.8 km) of a funnel cloud. At this distance, it can gather data close to a tornado if one forms.

3 miles (4.8 km)

Radio-controlled unmanned planes fly in the storm. They collect weather data from different locations above the ground.

Mesonets are vehicles with weather sensors on top of their roofs. They can report data in real time.

The long-band radar truck stays about 6 miles (9.7 km) away from the storm. From this distance, it can get a good view of the entire system. Like the other Vortex2 radar systems, it is very sensitive. Scientists can use it to tell tornado debris from precipitation.

The rapid-scan radar truck provides updated data about every seven seconds. It can produce 3-D radar images.

The crew in the field coordinator unit study weather maps and other data. They send out the data to other team leaders in the field.

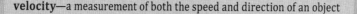

6 miles (9.7 km)

velocity—a measurement of both the speed and direction of an object

HOW TO HUNT A HURRICANE

The NOAA and Air Force Reserve hurricane hunters fly a triangular pattern called the alpha pattern through a hurricane. This pattern is repeated two times during a flight. It allows them to fly through the eye at least four times.

Fact:

Hurricanes in the northern hemisphere move in a counterclockwise direction. For this reason, the pilots always make left turns. The pattern allows the plane to fly with the winds instead of against them.

QUESTION: How has the NOAA Hurricane Hunters' research benefited science?

ANSWER: Hurricanes are now forecast with good accuracy at five days out from landfall. This gives people plenty of time to plan for orderly evacuation. We've also developed the technology to detect surface winds from NOAA aircraft, something that is very important to ship [crews] and homeowners near the coast.

Hurricane Allen sends waves crashing onto the Texas coast in 1980. This Category 5 hurricane caused severe damage.

BEHIND THE SCENES

Storm chasing is considered fieldwork. That's because the chasers gather data in the middle of the action. For hobbyists such as photographers, a lot of the work might be over after the chase. But for scientists, the work has only just begun. The data gathered by the weather instruments has to be studied in a lab. Many labs perform these tasks. Two of the major U.S. labs are the National Hurricane Center in Miami, Florida, and the National Severe Storms Laboratory in Norman, Oklahoma.

A Typical Day at the
NATIONAL HURRICANE CENTER
during Hurricane Season

1. Meteorologists arrive early to get updates on the current status of the storm.

2. The scientists begin looking over the radar images and the data from the NOAA and Air Force Reserve hurricane hunters.

3. First, the path of the hurricane is determined. Then the information is sent to computers in Washington, D.C. Computer models are made of the storm.

4. The meteorologists make preliminary forecasts and later final forecasts.

5. Once they have the final forecasts, scientists at the National Hurricane Center notify organizations that warn the public. These organizations include the National Weather Service, the U.S. Navy, and storm centers in other countries. The people in these offices warn the public.

6. As data continues to come in, the forecasts are constantly reviewed and updated.

Working at the
NATIONAL SEVERE STORMS LABORATORY (NSSL)

Only about 15 percent of researchers at the NSSL do fieldwork. And the ones who do fieldwork go out into the field less than 10 percent of the time. Most of the time, they study data already captured.

When data is brought in from a chase, researchers in a lab have to answer a lot of questions. First, they have to know how the data was collected. Was it on a moving vehicle? Or was it on the ground? Did other things affect the data, like wind or rain?

This process takes a lot of time. "You must be extremely patient to be a scientist. You can't make conclusions based on data with errors," says Susan Cobb, a meteorologist at the NSSL.

Once scientists know how the data was gathered, they start studying it. They try to re-create the storm on a computer. This computer model helps the scientists see how the storm would react if different factors were changed.

Scientists use the storm chase data to improve future forecasts. Sometimes they even use the data to make new equipment to use in field research. In 2011 the NSSL team invented a special balloon instrument. The scientists attached various instruments and cameras to it. They used the balloon to study conditions inside a storm. As the balloon rose, the instruments recorded how rain changed with altitude.

ON THE CHASE

Here's the inside scoop on what it's really like to be a storm chaser—from the mouths of the storm chasers themselves!

Why did you decide to become a storm chaser?

Rebekah LaBar: "When I was 12 years old, I saw my first tornado. The tornado was weak, but it moved right past my family's farm in Washington, which really scared me. At the same time I was fascinated by the storm, and decided I wanted to learn all I could about tornadoes so I wouldn't be as scared if I saw another one. When I was in college, I spent a summer in Oklahoma studying meteorology, and one of the students took me on my first storm chase. I was immediately hooked, and decided to go to graduate school in Oklahoma so that I could go storm chasing in my free time. I have now been storm chasing for eight years, since 2004."

What has been your most memorable experience as a storm chaser?

Josh Wurman: "The first significant tornado that I ever observed with a Doppler On Wheels was probably the most memorable. I got my very new, literally duct-taped together, DOW radar close to a major tornado crossing Dimmitt, Texas. I was able to see inside the tornado to map out the tremendous winds inside ... It was the moment of discovery, and one of the most memorable moments of my life."

Vacationing with a Storm

While some people camp or go to beaches on their vacations, others chase storms. A number of tour companies make it easy for beginners to experience storm chasing. Many of these companies put on tours in the heart of Tornado Alley.

Each tour chase is different because the groups encounter different weather. Sometimes tour groups get to see amazing lightning. The really lucky tour groups get to see supercells. And the even luckier ones get to see tornadoes. Sometimes, though, chasers will see very little but blue skies. The tour operators may take groups across the Great Plains to storm chasing landmarks. One afternoon might be spent at the Storm Prediction Center in Norman, Oklahoma. Another evening could be spent dining at places where storm chasers are known to hang out.

Jack Parrish:

What is your advice to kids who'd like to be a hurricane hunter someday?

"Studying meteorology takes a lot of math, science, and technology in school. Some of the classes I had to pass were no fun, and it wasn't always clear why I needed to study material that was so hard. But it led to a magical place out there in the sky, where teams of NOAA professionals do what seems impossible and almost make it look routine. If you like marine and atmospheric sciences, from fish to mammals to meteorology, keep NOAA in mind as a very cool career.

a storm chasing tour group in North Dakota

Chapter 4

SAFETY IN STORM CHASING

A tornado barrels toward a storm chaser's SUV in South Dakota.

Too Close For Comfort

Storm chasers sometimes get a lot closer to severe weather than they ever want to or expect. Sometimes these close calls are because of forecasting errors. Other times chasers make unwise decisions. In other cases, the chasers just find themselves in the wrong place at the wrong time.

A storm chase on May 29, 2004, took an unexpected turn for Chris McBee and his team. They were driving down a road near Piedmont, Oklahoma, chasing a tornado. Suddenly, the twister shifted directions and started heading directly for them. Chris hurriedly made a U-turn and sped back the way they had come. But there wasn't enough space between them and the tornado. The tornado's outer winds blew them off the road twice.

Fortunately, they eventually got to safety. "This was a very scary moment," Chris admits. Since then, Chris updated the equipment in his car. He is now better able to predict the paths of storms and tornadoes.

STAYING SAFE

Storm chasers are involved in a risky business. Danger can come from the storm itself or conditions the storm causes. And sometimes dangerous conditions come from the actions of the storm chasers. These safety guidelines are important for all chasers to follow:

1 Avoid chasing alone. Four eyes are better than two! When there are two people in a car, one person can watch the road. The other person can watch for tornadoes and check the forecasts. If someone is new to chasing, he or she should choose an experienced chasing partner.

2 Avoid chasing at night. When it's dark, chasers put themselves in serious danger because they can't see a storm.

3 Don't get caught up in the chase. Chasers sometimes get so excited about a storm that they forget to follow safe practices.

4 If in doubt, stay inside. If a situation looks a little too dangerous, chasers should stay inside their cars. Large hail can cause injuries, and lightning is also very dangerous.

DEBUNKING TORNADO MYTHS

MYTH: Highway overpasses are safe places to ride out a storm.

FACT: The overpass can act like a wind tunnel, sucking in debris. The debris then flies through the overpass quickly.

MYTH: Tornadoes do not strike in the mountains or in areas surrounded by mountains.

FACT: Tornadoes can strike any type of terrain. In 1999 an F2 tornado barreled through downtown Salt Lake City, Utah, a city surrounded by mountains.

MYTH: People can outrun tornadoes in a vehicle.

FACT: Tornadoes can move at speeds up to 70 miles (113 km) per hour. They also follow unpredictable paths. A person could end up traveling right into a tornado's path instead of away from it.

5 Obey the law. The number one chasing hazard is unsafe driving. Storm chasers are expected to follow the rules of the road.

6 Have an exit plan. Storm chasers should always have an escape plan if they get too close to a storm. At what point do they need to bail? Which direction should they go? Storm chasers should always make sure that they have a way to get out too. They should not let their vehicles get blocked in by other vehicles. They also shouldn't walk a far distance from their vehicles or park on a dead-end road.

SEEING DESTRUCTION FIRSTHAND

A group of storm chasers is hot on the path of a tornado. They have just filmed it from a distance. They hope that the twister hasn't caused any damage to people or property. But as they drive closer, their greatest fears have been realized. All that remains of a once thriving town is a path of destruction. Power lines crisscross the ground. People wander across piles of rubble that were once their homes. Others lie injured under fallen roofs.

Reed Timmer (front) and his team chase the EF4 tornado that hit Yazoo City, Mississippi, in 2010.

Storm chasers are heartsick when they see destruction that a tornado caused. Storm chaser Rebekah LaBar saw the damage from a tornado that hit Greensburg, Kansas, in 2007. She said, "... it shook me up so badly, I quit storm chasing for a year. I reevaluated why I storm chase and then started to make more of an effort to report all severe weather I saw to the National Weather Service ..."

Many chasers promise to themselves that they will stop and help if they come across an area struck by a tornado. On April 24, 2010, a tornado struck Yazoo City, Mississippi. Storm chaser Reed Timmer and his team came across the destruction the tornado had caused. This chase appeared on the "Why We Chase" episode of Discovery Channel's *Storm Chasers*. The storm chasers were some of the first responders to the scene. They had to carefully navigate through the rubble. They crossed downed power lines and avoided natural gas leaks. They carefully walked around buildings that were about to collapse. Along with their medic, the group helped people who were injured and trapped in the wreckage.

damage from the EF5 tornado that hit Greensburg, Kansas, in 2007

Seeing the damage from a storm helps many chasers refocus their efforts. They know if they can learn more about how tornadoes form, they can improve warning lead times. According to the NSSL, the average lead time for tornadoes is 11 minutes. This is often not enough time for people to find safety. With better lead times, property will still be damaged. But property can be replaced, while lives cannot.

Q & A WITH STORM CHASER CHRIS McBEE

QUESTION: What future goals do you have for storm chasing?

ANSWER: One goal I have is to purchase several weather radios to give to people I encounter on chases, especially those in very rural areas. Five hundred fifty-one people died in the U.S. in tornadoes in 2011 alone. Some of those people were unaware of the weather situation and did not get themselves into a safe place. I plan to do what little I can to turn that situation around and ultimately try to save some lives.

Glossary

air pressure (AYR PRESH-ur)—force exerted by the weight of the molecules that make up air; usually, the lower the air pressure, the stronger the storm

altitude (AL-ti-tood)—the height of something above sea level or Earth's surface

atmosphere (AT-muhss-fihr)—the mixture of gases that surrounds Earth

condense (kuhn-DENS)—to change from a gas to a liquid

evaporate (i-VA-puh-rayt)—to change from a liquid into a vapor or a gas

eye (EYE)—the calm, clear zone at the center of a hurricane

eyewall (eye-WAL)—a tall, vertical wall of fast-moving clouds surrounding a hurricane's eye

funnel cloud (FUHN-uhl KLOUD)—a cloud that hangs from a larger storm cloud but has not touched the ground; funnel clouds often have rotation and precede a tornado

GPS—an electronic tool that uses satellites to find the location of objects; GPS stands for Global Positioning System

hemisphere (HEM-uhss-fihr)—one half of the Earth; the equator divides the Earth into northern and southern hemispheres

humidity (hyoo-MIH-du-tee)—the measure of the moisture in the air

meteorologist (mee-tee-ur-AWL-uh-jist)—a person who studies and predicts the weather

radar (RAY-dar)—a device that uses radio waves to track the location of objects

relative humidity (REL-uh-tiv hyoo-MIH-du-tee)—the ratio of the amount of water vapor present in the air to the maximum amount that can exist in vapor form at that specific temperature and pressure

satellite (SAT-uh-lite)—a spacecraft that circles Earth; satellites take pictures of Earth from space

tornado (tor-NAY-doh)—a violent spinning column of air that makes contact with the ground

velocity (vuh-LOSS-uh-tee)—a measurement of both the speed and direction of an object

Read More

Carson, Mary Kay. *Inside Weather.* Inside Series. New York: Sterling Children's Books, 2011.

Dougherty, Terri. *Anatomy of a Tornado.* Disasters. Mankato, Minn.: Capstone Press, 2011.

Rajczak, Kristen. *Terrifying Tornadoes.* Angry Earth. New York: Gareth Stevens Pub., 2012.

Raum, Elizabeth. *Can You Survive Storm Chasing?: An Interactive Survival Adventure.* You Choose: Survival. Mankato, Minn.: Capstone Press, 2012.

Internet Sites

FactHound offers a safe, fun way to find Internet sites related to this book. All of the sites on FactHound have been researched by our staff.

Here's all you do:

Visit *www.facthound.com*

Type in this code: 9781429699846

Index